Handbook for the Roaring 2020s

"How to Generate Wealth in the New Age"

Introduction

The echoes of history often reverberate through time, offering us valuable insights into the present and the future. Just over a century ago, the world witnessed a remarkable period known as the Roaring Twenties. It was an era of unparalleled economic growth, cultural dynamism, and financial opportunity. Yet, like all booms, it was not without its pitfalls.

Fast forward to today, and we find ourselves in the midst of the Roaring 2020s, a new era characterized by rapid technological advancement, global interconnectedness, and unprecedented opportunities for wealth creation. The parallels between the two decades are uncanny, and they beckon us to draw lessons from the past while embracing the unique opportunities of the present.

In "Generating Wealth in the Roaring 2020s," we embark on a journey to explore the economic landscape of the 21st century and uncover the pathways to financial success in this exciting era. We'll draw upon the experiences of the Roaring Twenties, examining the triumphs and tribulations of those who navigated the soaring markets, extravagant lifestyles, and societal transformations of that time.

But this book is not merely a history lesson. It is a practical guide for individuals seeking to thrive in today's ever-evolving economy. We'll dive deep into the strategies, mindsets, and actions that can propel you towards financial prosperity, just as the pioneers of the 1920s seized their opportunities.

In the pages that follow, you'll discover how to adapt to the demands of the new generation, harness the power of technology, and capitalize on the global marketplace. Whether you're an aspiring entrepreneur, an investor looking for the next big thing, or someone exploring the possibilities of the gig economy, there's a wealth-building strategy waiting for you.

The Roaring 2020s have dawned, and the world is brimming with potential for those who are prepared to seize it. As we embark on this journey together, remember that the road to wealth is not just about money; it's about knowledge, resilience, and the determination to shape your financial destiny.

So, let's step into this exciting decade, learn from the past, embrace the present, and chart a course towards prosperity in the Roaring 2020s.

Chapter 1: Economic Parallels

As we delve into the dynamics of wealth generation in the Roaring 2020s, it's essential to establish a firm understanding of the economic parallels that connect this era to its predecessor, the Roaring Twenties. By recognizing these similarities and differences, we can gain valuable insights into the opportunities and challenges that lie ahead.

The New Roaring Twenties: A Century Apart

The 1920s was an era of exuberance and economic growth. A post-World War I period, it saw a surge in industrialization, urbanization, and consumerism. Advances in technology, like the automobile and radio, revolutionized daily life, while the stock market reached unprecedented heights. Society was marked by an embrace of modernity, with cultural shifts and the emergence of new industries contributing to an air of optimism.

Fast forward to today, and the 2020s have begun with a similar sense of hope and transformation. The rapid pace of technological innovation, epitomized by the internet and smartphones, has reshaped our world. Globalization has deepened, allowing for the seamless exchange of goods, services, and ideas across borders. The digital age has democratized entrepreneurship, making it easier for individuals to start businesses and reach global audiences. However, like the 1920s, the Roaring 2020s come with their own unique challenges. Inequalities have widened, and societal issues such as climate change and cybersecurity demand our attention. The interconnectedness of our global economy means that economic shocks can ripple across the world in mere seconds. To navigate this complex landscape successfully, we must learn from history while adapting to the demands of our time.

The Resilience of Innovation

One striking parallel between the two decades is the role of innovation as a driving force behind economic growth. In the 1920s, innovations in manufacturing, transportation, and communication propelled the economy forward. Similarly, today's digital revolution, characterized by artificial intelligence, blockchain, and biotechnology, is reshaping industries and creating new opportunities.

In both eras, those who recognized the potential of innovative technologies were poised to benefit the most. The Roaring 2020s, like the Roaring Twenties, reward those who embrace change, think creatively, and adapt to emerging trends.

Globalization and the New Marketplaces

Another significant parallel is the expansion of global markets. The 1920s saw the growth of international trade, with American products reaching consumers worldwide. Today, the internet has turned the world into a vast marketplace, where entrepreneurs and businesses can connect with customers, suppliers, and partners on a global scale.

Whether you're a small-town artisan or a tech-savvy startup founder, your potential audience is no longer limited by geography. Understanding how to tap into these global opportunities will be a key theme in our exploration of wealth generation strategies.

As we embark on this journey through the Roaring 2020s, keep these economic parallels in mind. They serve as a backdrop for the wealth-building strategies and insights that will follow in the subsequent chapters. In the pages ahead, we'll delve deeper into the lessons we can glean from the past and the strategies that can pave the way to prosperity in this new era of wealth creation.

Chapter 2: Lessons from the Past

History is a remarkable teacher, offering us invaluable insights into the choices and consequences of those who came before us. In this chapter, we'll delve into the Roaring Twenties to uncover the lessons—both cautionary and inspiring—that can guide us in navigating the Roaring 2020s.

The Roaring Twenties: A Tale of Prosperity and Excess

The 1920s was a time of unprecedented economic prosperity in the United States and many other parts of the world. The end of World War I brought about a sense of relief and optimism, and this was reflected in a booming economy. Industrial production soared, consumer spending rose, and the stock market reached dizzying heights. The era became known for its extravagant parties, Jazz Age culture, and the emergence of a more liberated lifestyle.
However, this prosperity was not without its dark side. The stock market crash of 1929 and the

subsequent Great Depression demonstrated the fragility of this seemingly invincible economy. The excesses of the Roaring Twenties gave way to a sobering reality, where many faced financial ruin.

Lessons from the Roaring Twenties

1. The Power of Innovation: The 1920s were marked by innovations like the assembly line, which revolutionized manufacturing, and the radio, which transformed communication. Today, technological innovations continue to shape our world. As we navigate the Roaring 2020s, it's crucial to recognize the potential of emerging technologies and industries.
2. The Importance of Diversification: The stock market crash of 1929 serves as a stark reminder of the risks associated with putting all your eggs in one basket. Diversification—spreading investments across different assets—is a lesson that remains as relevant today as it was then.
3. The Impact of Speculation: The Roaring Twenties saw rampant speculation in the stock market, with many investors buying stocks on margin (borrowed money). This speculative frenzy ultimately led to the crash. Avoiding excessive risk-taking and maintaining a prudent approach to investments is a lesson we should heed.
4. Financial Preparedness: The Great Depression exposed the importance of having a financial safety

net. Building an emergency fund and practicing responsible financial management can help protect your wealth in times of economic uncertainty.

5. Adaptability: The survivors of the Great Depression were often those who could adapt to changing circumstances. In the Roaring 2020s, where disruption is constant, adaptability remains a critical skill.

By learning from the successes and failures of the past, we can navigate the Roaring 2020s with a greater sense of purpose and preparedness. In the chapters ahead, we'll explore how these lessons can be applied to seize the opportunities and address the challenges of today's ever-evolving economic landscape. Whether you're an aspiring entrepreneur, an investor, or someone looking to build wealth in the gig economy, these historical insights will provide a solid foundation for your financial journey.

Chapter 3: Today's Economic Landscape

Understanding the present economic landscape is essential as we embark on our journey to generate wealth in the Roaring 2020s. In this chapter, we'll examine the factors and forces that shape our current environment, setting the stage for the strategies and opportunities we'll explore in the subsequent chapters.

The Digital Transformation

At the heart of today's economic landscape is the digital revolution. The advent of the internet and the proliferation of smartphones have fundamentally changed the way we live, work, and do business. Here are some key aspects to consider:

Digital Connectivity: The internet has connected billions of people worldwide, creating a vast global marketplace. This connectivity has reduced barriers to entry for entrepreneurs and expanded the reach of businesses.

E-commerce: Online shopping has surged, and platforms like Amazon and Alibaba have become retail giants. Whether you're a seller or a consumer, e-commerce has reshaped how goods are bought and sold.

Remote Work: The rise of remote work has made it possible for people to work from anywhere. This shift in the workforce has implications for both employees and entrepreneurs.

Digital Payment and Cryptocurrency: Digital currencies like Bitcoin and Ethereum are challenging traditional financial systems.

Understanding these emerging technologies is crucial for those seeking to navigate the financial landscape of the Roaring 2020s.

The Gig Economy and Entrepreneurship

In the Roaring 2020s, traditional employment models are evolving. The gig economy, characterized by short-term contracts and freelance work, is on the rise. Entrepreneurship has also become more accessible, thanks to digital tools and platforms that empower individuals to start businesses with minimal upfront costs.

Freelancing: The gig economy offers opportunities for those with specialized skills to work independently and on their terms. We'll explore strategies for thriving in this dynamic environment.

Entrepreneurship: The barriers to entrepreneurship have never been lower. Whether you're launching a tech startup or a local service business, we'll discuss the essential steps for success.

Globalization and Market Access

The world is more interconnected than ever before. Globalization has opened up new markets and customer bases, allowing businesses of all sizes to reach a global audience. However, it also means increased competition and the need to understand diverse markets and cultures.

Market Expansion: We'll explore how businesses can tap into international markets and navigate the complexities of global trade. Market Research: Understanding consumer preferences and trends on a global scale is essential for businesses looking to expand their reach.

As we navigate the Roaring 2020s, it's clear that our economic landscape is characterized by rapid change and unprecedented opportunities. In the chapters that follow, we'll delve into specific wealth-building strategies, drawing on the lessons of history and the dynamics of today's economy. Whether you're an investor, an aspiring entrepreneur, or someone seeking to thrive in the gig economy, understanding this economic landscape will be instrumental in your pursuit of financial success.

Chapter 4: Adapting to the New Generation

In the Roaring 2020s, success is not solely about your financial investments; it's about investing in yourself and your ability to adapt to the ever-changing landscape. This chapter explores the mindset and skills needed to thrive in this new era, where agility and continuous learning are paramount.

The Power of Adaptability

Adaptability is the cornerstone of success in the Roaring 2020s. Here's why it matters:

Rapid Technological Advancement: Technology evolves at breakneck speed. Being adaptable means staying up-to-date with the latest trends and tools in your field.

Changing Work Environments: The rise of remote work, the gig economy, and flexible job arrangements requires individuals to adapt to new ways of working and collaborating.

Global Competition: As markets become more globalized, businesses and professionals must adapt to compete on a broader scale and with a diverse set of competitors.

Continuous Learning and Skill Development

Lifelong Learning: The ability to learn and unlearn is a skill in itself. Embrace a mindset of continuous learning, whether through formal education, online courses, or self-study.

Skill Diversification: The more skills you acquire, the more adaptable you become. Consider developing both hard and soft skills to remain versatile in a changing job market.

Tech Literacy: In the digital age, being tech-savvy is crucial. Even if you're not in a tech-related field, understanding technology can give you an edge in various industries.

Embracing Risk and Failure

Risk-Taking: The Roaring 2020s reward calculated risk-taking. Whether you're an entrepreneur or an investor, embracing some level of risk is often necessary for substantial rewards.

Learning from Failure: Failure is not the end; it's a stepping stone to success. Emulate the resilience of entrepreneurs who learn from their failures and use them as opportunities to grow.

Cultivating an Entrepreneurial Mindset

Innovation: Think like an entrepreneur, even if you're not starting a business. Innovate within your job, industry, or personal projects to stay relevant.

Problem-Solving: Entrepreneurship is about solving problems. Identify issues in your field or market and work on creative solutions.

Networking: Building a strong network is vital. Collaborate with others, share ideas, and seek mentors who can guide you on your path to success.

Adapt to Market Trends: Keep a keen eye on market trends, customer behavior, and emerging technologies. Pivot and adapt your strategies as needed.

As we journey through the Roaring 2020s, remember that success is not only about seizing opportunities but also about preparing yourself to thrive in a rapidly evolving world. By embracing adaptability, continuous learning, and an entrepreneurial mindset, you'll be well-equipped to navigate the challenges and seize the opportunities of this exciting era of wealth creation. In the chapters that follow, we'll explore specific wealth-building strategies that align with these principles, helping you forge your path to financial success.

Chapter 5: Entrepreneurship in the Digital Age

As we dive deeper into strategies for wealth generation in the Roaring 2020s, one avenue stands out prominently: entrepreneurship. This chapter explores the world of entrepreneurship in the digital age, where innovation, agility, and creativity are the keys to success.

The Entrepreneurial Ecosystem

In today's interconnected world, entrepreneurship has evolved into a vibrant ecosystem. Here are some key aspects to consider:

Startups and Innovation: The startup culture is thriving, with innovators and disruptors challenging established industries. Entrepreneurs are launching businesses across a spectrum of sectors, from tech and e-commerce to sustainability and healthcare.

Access to Resources: The digital age has democratized access to resources. Funding is available through venture capital, crowdfunding, and angel investors. Incubators and accelerators provide mentorship and support. Global Reach: The internet allows startups to access a global customer base from day one. Businesses can scale rapidly and reach audiences that were previously out of reach.

Entrepreneurial Mindset and Skills

Vision and Innovation: Successful entrepreneurs have a clear vision and the ability to innovate. They identify problems or opportunities and develop creative solutions. Risk Management: Entrepreneurship involves risk, but effective entrepreneurs are skilled at managing and mitigating it. They make informed decisions and pivot when necessary. Resilience: Setbacks are part of the entrepreneurial journey. Resilience and the ability to learn from failure are crucial for long-term success. Adaptability: The ability to adapt to changing market conditions and customer needs is essential. Successful entrepreneurs are agile and responsive.

Starting Your Own Business

If you're considering entrepreneurship, here are some key steps to get started:

Identify Your Passion: Start by identifying your interests and passions. Building a business around something you're passionate about can be incredibly motivating.

Market Research: Research your target market thoroughly. Understand your potential customers, their needs, and your competition.

Business Plan: Create a detailed business plan outlining your goals, strategies, and financial projections. A well-thought-out plan is essential for attracting investors and guiding your business.

Funding: Explore funding options, including bootstrapping (self-funding), seeking investors, or crowdfunding. Choose the method that aligns with your business model.

Build a Team: Surround yourself with a talented and diverse team. Complementary skills and perspectives can be invaluable.

Launch and Iterate: Launch your business, gather feedback, and iterate on your product or service based on customer input.

Scale: Once your business gains traction, focus on scaling and expanding your reach.

Remember that entrepreneurship is a journey filled with challenges and rewards. Success may not come overnight, but with dedication and the right approach, you can build a thriving business in the Roaring 2020s.

In the chapters that follow, we'll continue to explore additional wealth-building strategies, including investment opportunities, freelancing, and leveraging digital tools to maximize your financial potential in this dynamic era. Whether you're an aspiring entrepreneur or someone seeking alternative wealth-building avenues, the Roaring 2020s offer a wealth of possibilities for those willing to take the leap.

Chapter 6: Investing in the Digital Age

Investing has long been a cornerstone of wealth creation, and in the Roaring 2020s, it remains as relevant and promising as ever. This chapter explores the world of investment in today's digital age, where technology has transformed how we access and manage our financial assets.

The Digital Investment Landscape

The Roaring 2020s have witnessed significant changes in how people invest and manage their money. Key aspects of the digital investment landscape include:

Online Brokerages: Traditional brick-and-mortar brokerages have given way to online platforms that allow individuals to trade stocks, bonds, and other assets with ease and at lower costs.

Robo-Advisors: Robo-advisors leverage artificial intelligence to offer automated, low-cost investment management services. They create diversified portfolios based on an investor's risk tolerance and financial goals.

Cryptocurrencies: The rise of digital currencies like Bitcoin and Ethereum has introduced a new asset class to the investment world. These assets can offer both substantial opportunities and risks.

Crowdfunding and P2P Lending: Online platforms facilitate crowdfunding investments in startups, real estate, and other ventures. Peer-to-peer lending platforms allow individuals to lend money directly to borrowers, potentially earning interest in return.

Investment Strategies for the Digital Age

Diversification: Diversifying your investment portfolio across various asset classes can help manage risk. This principle remains fundamental in the digital age.

Research and Due Diligence: Conduct thorough research before making investment decisions. Whether you're investing in stocks, cryptocurrencies, or startups, knowledge is your most potent weapon.

Risk Management: Understand your risk tolerance and invest accordingly. Diversification, as well as tools like stop-loss orders, can help mitigate risk.

Long-Term Perspective: The Roaring 2020s may bring volatility, but maintaining a long-term perspective can help you weather market fluctuations and capitalize on compound returns.

Leverage Technology: Embrace technology to streamline your investment process. Online tools, mobile apps, and investment platforms can provide real-time data and insights to inform your decisions.

Investment Opportunities

Stock Market: Traditional stocks and exchange-traded funds (ETFs) remain popular investment options. Consider investing in companies that align with your values and have strong growth potential.

Real Estate: Real estate investment trusts (REITs) and crowdfunding platforms offer opportunities to invest in real estate without the hassle of property management.

Cryptocurrencies: While cryptocurrencies are highly speculative, they have gained traction as a legitimate asset class. Educate yourself and invest only what you can afford to lose.

Startups: Participating in equity crowdfunding or investing in startups through online platforms can be a way to support innovation and potentially reap substantial rewards.

In the Roaring 2020s, investing is not limited to Wall Street; it's accessible to anyone with an internet connection. However, with greater accessibility comes greater responsibility. Make informed decisions, stay vigilant, and continuously educate yourself about the ever-evolving investment landscape. The Roaring 2020s are filled with investment opportunities, but success requires diligence and a clear strategy to build and protect your wealth.

Chapter 7: Thriving in the Gig Economy

The gig economy, characterized by short-term contracts, freelance work, and independent contracting, has become a dominant force in the Roaring 2020s. This chapter explores how to navigate and prosper in this dynamic and flexible work environment.

The Gig Economy: A New Way of Working

The gig economy represents a fundamental shift in the way people work and earn income. Key features include:

Flexibility: Workers have greater control over their schedules, choosing when and where they work. This flexibility can be especially appealing for those seeking work-life balance.

Diverse Opportunities: Gig work spans a wide range of industries, from ride-sharing and food delivery to writing, design, and programming. Virtually any skill can be monetized.

Entrepreneurial Spirit: Gig workers often function as micro-entrepreneurs, managing their businesses, marketing their services, and building their brand.

Strategies for Success in the Gig Economy

Identify Your Niche: Determine your unique skills and expertise. What can you offer that sets you apart from the competition? Focus on niches where your talents shine.

Build Your Brand: As a gig worker, your personal brand is your most valuable asset. Develop a professional online presence through a portfolio website, social media, and networking.

Marketing and Self-Promotion: Promote your services to potential clients or customers. Leverage online marketing tools and platforms to reach a broader audience.

Pricing and Negotiation: Set fair prices for your services while considering market rates. Be prepared to negotiate and communicate your value effectively.

Client Relationships: Provide exceptional customer service to build long-term client relationships. Satisfied clients are more likely to provide repeat business and referrals.

Financial Management in the Gig Economy

Budgeting: Create a budget to manage your income and expenses effectively. Since gig work can have irregular income, budgeting is crucial for financial stability.

Tax Planning: Understand your tax obligations as a gig worker. Set aside a portion of your earnings for taxes and consider working with a tax professional.

Savings and Retirement: In the absence of employer-sponsored retirement plans, set up your own retirement savings accounts, such as a solo 401(k) or a SEP IRA.

Insurance: Gig workers may not have access to traditional employee benefits. Explore options for health, disability, and liability insurance to protect yourself and your business.

The gig economy offers immense potential for those seeking autonomy, flexibility, and the opportunity to capitalize on their skills and passions. However, success in this arena requires careful planning, dedication, and a strong entrepreneurial spirit. By adopting these strategies and embracing the gig economy's unique opportunities, you can thrive and build your wealth in the Roaring 2020s.

Chapter 8: Digital Tools for Financial Success

In the Roaring 2020s, technology plays a pivotal role in shaping our financial landscape. This chapter explores the digital tools and resources available to individuals seeking financial success in an increasingly connected world.

The Digital Transformation of Finance

The digital revolution has ushered in a new era of financial management and opportunities. Here are some key aspects to consider:

Online Banking: Traditional brick-and-mortar banks have been complemented (and in some cases, replaced) by online banks and financial apps, offering convenience and often higher interest rates.

Mobile Payment Apps: Payment apps like PayPal, Venmo, and Cash App have revolutionized the way we handle transactions, making it easier to send money and make payments on the go.

Personal Finance Apps: A plethora of personal finance apps are available, helping individuals budget, save, invest, and track their financial goals with precision.

Investment Platforms: Online investment platforms, robo-advisors, and trading apps provide accessibility to a wide range of investment opportunities, often with lower fees.

Cryptocurrency Wallets: Digital wallets allow individuals to securely store and manage cryptocurrencies, facilitating participation in the growing digital currency market.

Using Digital Tools to Maximize Financial Success

Budgeting and Expense Tracking: Apps like Mint, YNAB (You Need A Budget), and PocketGuard help you create and stick to a budget by tracking income and expenses in real-time.

Investment Platforms: Platforms like Robinhood, Wealthfront, and Betterment offer easy access to stocks, bonds, and other investment options with user-friendly interfaces.

Cryptocurrency Wallets: For those interested in digital currencies, wallets like Coinbase and Ledger provide secure storage and management of cryptocurrencies.

Online Tax Filing: Platforms like TurboTax and H&R Block make tax preparation and filing

straightforward, ensuring you take advantage of potential deductions.
Financial Education: Digital tools also provide access to financial education resources, including online courses, webinars, and forums, to enhance your financial literacy.

Security and Privacy Considerations

With the convenience of digital tools comes the need for vigilance in ensuring your financial information remains secure:

Strong Passwords: Use complex, unique passwords for financial accounts, and consider using a password manager to keep track of them.

Two-Factor Authentication: Enable two-factor authentication wherever possible to add an extra layer of security to your accounts.

Data Encryption: Ensure that financial apps and websites you use employ robust encryption protocols to protect your data.

Regular Updates: Keep your devices and apps up to date to benefit from the latest security patches.

Be Wary of Scams: Be cautious of phishing emails, fraudulent websites, and unsolicited requests for personal information.

The Roaring 2020s provide an abundance of digital tools and resources to help you take control of your finances, make informed decisions, and work toward your financial goals. By harnessing these tools and maintaining a strong commitment to security, you can position yourself for financial success in this tech-driven era.

Chapter 9: Real Estate in the Digital Age

Real estate has long been a cornerstone of wealth creation, and in the Roaring 2020s, the digital age has transformed the way we buy, sell, invest, and manage property. This chapter explores the opportunities and strategies for success in the ever-evolving world of real estate.

Digital Transformation of Real Estate

The digital age has revolutionized the real estate industry in several key ways:

Online Property Search: Homebuyers and investors can access vast databases of property listings, complete with photos, videos, and detailed descriptions, making it easier to identify potential investments.

Virtual Tours: Virtual reality (VR) and augmented reality (AR) technologies allow for immersive virtual property tours, reducing the need for physical visits.

Real Estate Marketplaces: Online marketplaces like Zillow, Redfin, and Realtor.com provide up-to-date market data, property insights, and tools for buyers, sellers, and investors.

Property Management Software: Landlords and property managers use digital platforms to streamline rent collection, maintenance requests, and tenant communication.

Real Estate Crowdfunding: Online platforms enable individuals to invest in real estate properties collectively, reducing the barrier to entry for property investment.

Strategies for Real Estate Success

Whether you're looking to buy your first home, invest in rental properties, or explore commercial real estate, these strategies can help you succeed in the digital age:

Educate Yourself: Understand the fundamentals of real estate, including property types, financing options, and market analysis.

Online courses and resources can provide valuable knowledge.

Leverage Online Tools: Use online real estate marketplaces to search for properties, analyze market trends, and access financial calculators to evaluate potential investments.

Build a Real Estate Team: Collaborate with real estate agents, lenders, inspectors, and contractors who have a strong online presence and can help you navigate the digital landscape.

Property Due Diligence: Conduct thorough research on properties of interest, including inspection reports, title searches, and historical data on rental income and expenses.

Consider Real Estate Crowdfunding: Explore real estate crowdfunding platforms if you want to invest in properties without the responsibility of direct ownership and management.

Real Estate Investment Trusts (REITs): REITs provide a way to invest in real estate assets without purchasing physical properties. They offer liquidity and diversification.

Real Estate in the Digital Age: Challenges and Opportunities

While the digital age has brought unprecedented convenience and access to real estate information, it also presents challenges:

Competition: The ease of online property search means increased competition for desirable properties, potentially driving up prices.

Data Privacy: Be cautious about sharing personal and financial information online, especially when engaging with real estate listings or contacting agents.

Market Volatility: Digital tools provide real-time market data, but they can also contribute to market volatility and speculation.

Property Scams: Be vigilant for online property scams, including fraudulent listings or rental scams. Verify information and work with reputable professionals.

The digital transformation of real estate offers abundant opportunities for those who navigate this dynamic landscape effectively. By leveraging online resources, building a strong real estate team, and conducting thorough due diligence, you can harness the power of the digital age to create wealth through real estate in the Roaring 2020s.

Chapter 10: Sustainable Investing for the Future

In the Roaring 2020s, a new era of investing has emerged—one that not only seeks financial returns but also promotes positive environmental and social impact. This chapter explores sustainable investing, where aligning your investments with your values can lead to both financial and societal benefits.

The Rise of Sustainable Investing

Sustainable investing, also known as ESG (Environmental, Social, and Governance) investing, integrates environmental, social, and ethical factors into the investment decision-making process. Here's why it's gaining prominence:

Environmental Impact: Climate change and environmental issues have become critical global concerns. Sustainable investing aims to support businesses and initiatives that promote environmental sustainability.

Social Responsibility: Investors increasingly consider the societal impact of their investments, supporting companies that

prioritize fair labor practices, diversity, and community engagement.
Corporate Governance: Governance factors, such as transparent management practices and ethical decision-making, contribute to long-term business stability and growth.

Sustainable Investment Strategies

ESG Integration: Incorporate ESG factors into your investment analysis. Look for companies with strong ESG performance and consider ESG-focused investment funds and indices.
Impact Investing: Directly invest in projects or companies that address specific social or environmental challenges, such as renewable energy, clean technology, or affordable housing.
Community Development Investing: Support local communities by investing in community development financial institutions (CDFIs) or projects that promote economic empowerment and revitalization.
Shareholder Engagement: Engage with companies as a shareholder to influence their policies and practices positively. Voting your proxies and participating in shareholder advocacy can make a difference.

Sustainable Funds: Invest in mutual funds or exchange-traded funds (ETFs) that focus on sustainable or ESG-related themes, allowing for diversification within the sustainable investment space.

Balancing Returns and Impact

Sustainable investing doesn't necessarily mean sacrificing financial returns. In fact, evidence suggests that companies with strong ESG performance can be more resilient and generate competitive returns over the long term.

Risk Mitigation: ESG factors can help identify potential risks such as environmental liabilities or governance issues that may affect a company's financial performance.

Consumer Preferences: As consumer preferences shift towards sustainable products and services, businesses that embrace sustainability may enjoy increased customer loyalty and market share.

Regulatory Trends: Governments and regulatory bodies are increasingly focusing on ESG disclosure and sustainable practices, making compliance an essential aspect of risk management.

Impact Measurement: Investors can track the positive outcomes of their sustainable investments, providing a sense of purpose and accountability.

Sustainability and Your Financial Goals

Sustainable investing offers the opportunity to align your investments with your values and contribute to a more sustainable and equitable world. However, it's essential to strike a balance between impact and financial returns, considering your long-term financial goals and risk tolerance.

As you explore sustainable investing in the Roaring 2020s, keep in mind that it's a dynamic field, with evolving standards and opportunities. By integrating sustainability into your investment strategy, you can build wealth while making a positive difference in the world, aligning your financial success with a brighter future for all.

Chapter 11: The Future of Wealth Generation

As we near the end of this journey through the Roaring 2020s and the strategies for wealth generation in this dynamic era, it's essential to reflect on the future of wealth creation and the evolving landscape of finance, business, and technology.

Emerging Trends and Challenges

Artificial Intelligence and Automation: AI and automation will continue to reshape industries, from manufacturing to finance. Investing in AI-driven companies and understanding how automation impacts your career or business is essential.

Sustainability and Impact: Sustainable and impact investing will become more mainstream as consumers, businesses, and investors prioritize environmental and social responsibility.

Digital Currencies: The adoption of digital currencies, including central bank digital currencies (CBDCs), will disrupt traditional financial systems, offering new investment and payment opportunities.

Blockchain and Decentralization: Blockchain technology has the potential to revolutionize supply chains, voting systems, and financial transactions. Understanding blockchain and its applications can be valuable.

Remote Work and Gig Economy: The gig economy and remote work will continue to grow, impacting how people earn income and businesses operate. Adaptability and digital skills will be crucial.

Personal Finance and Financial Education

Financial Literacy: Ongoing financial education is vital as the financial landscape evolves. Stay informed about new investment opportunities, tax laws, and personal finance strategies.
Diversification: Continue to diversify your investments across asset classes and industries to manage risk effectively.
Emergency Savings: Maintain a robust emergency fund to weather unexpected financial challenges.
Retirement Planning: Plan for retirement early and consistently contribute to retirement accounts, taking advantage of employer-sponsored plans and tax-advantaged options.
Estate Planning: Create a comprehensive estate plan, including wills, trusts, and healthcare directives, to protect your assets and ensure your wishes are met.

Adapting to Change

The Roaring 2020s have taught us that change is constant, and adaptability is a crucial skill. To thrive in the evolving landscape of wealth generation, consider these principles:

Lifelong Learning: Cultivate a mindset of continuous learning to stay relevant and adaptable in your career or business.

Networking: Build and maintain a diverse network of contacts who can provide insights, mentorship, and collaboration opportunities.

Resilience: Embrace setbacks as opportunities for growth and maintain a resilient outlook in the face of challenges.

Purposeful Investing: Align your investments and financial decisions with your values and long-term goals.

The Roaring 2020s have ushered in a period of remarkable change, offering unprecedented opportunities for wealth generation. Yet, with these opportunities come new responsibilities and challenges. By staying informed, embracing change, and making thoughtful financial choices, you can navigate this dynamic era with confidence and create a prosperous future for yourself and your loved ones. The journey to wealth generation continues, and your path is uniquely yours to shape.

Chapter 12: Your Wealth Journey Begins

As we conclude our exploration of wealth generation in the Roaring 2020s, it's time to embark on your personal wealth-building journey armed with knowledge, strategies, and a forward-looking perspective. This chapter provides practical steps to get started on the path to financial success.

Define Your Financial Goals

Short-Term Goals: Start by setting achievable short-term financial goals. These could include building an emergency fund, paying off high-interest debt, or saving for a vacation. Intermediate Goals: Look ahead to intermediate-term goals, such as buying a home, funding your children's education, or starting a business. Long-Term Goals: Plan for long-term objectives like retirement, financial independence, and leaving a legacy for future generations.

Create a Financial Plan

Budget: Establish a realistic budget to track your income and expenses. Use digital tools and apps to make budgeting easier and more effective.

Emergency Fund: Build an emergency fund with enough to cover three to six months' worth of living expenses. This provides financial security in case of unexpected events.

Debt Management: Develop a strategy to pay off high-interest debt systematically. Prioritize paying down credit card balances and other debts with high interest rates.

Investment Strategy: Determine your risk tolerance and investment goals. Create a diversified investment portfolio that aligns with your objectives, whether they're short-term or long-term.

Retirement Planning: Maximize contributions to retirement accounts like a 401(k) or an IRA. Take advantage of employer match programs and tax benefits for retirement savings.

Estate Planning: Consult with an estate planning attorney to create essential documents like a will, power of attorney, and healthcare directive. Review and update your estate plan regularly.

Educate Yourself Continuously

Read and Research: Stay informed about financial trends, investment opportunities, and personal finance strategies by reading books, articles, and news related to finance and economics.

Online Courses: Enroll in online courses or webinars to deepen your knowledge in specific financial areas, such as investing, tax planning, or retirement strategies.

Financial Advisors: Consider working with a financial advisor or planner who can provide personalized guidance and help you make informed financial decisions.

Take Action and Stay Disciplined

Automate Savings and Investments: Set up automatic transfers to your savings and investment accounts. This ensures consistent contributions without relying on willpower alone.

Monitor Your Progress: Regularly review your financial plan and adjust it as needed to accommodate changing circumstances or goals.

Stay Disciplined: Discipline and consistency are key to financial success. Avoid impulsive spending, and resist the urge to make hasty investment decisions during market fluctuations.

Stay Inspired and Motivated

Share Your Goals: Share your financial goals with a trusted friend or family member who can provide support and encouragement.

Celebrate Achievements: Celebrate milestones along your wealth-building journey, whether it's paying off debt, reaching a savings goal, or achieving a higher investment return.

Visualize Success: Create a vision board or visual reminders of your financial goals to keep you motivated and focused on your objectives.

Your journey to wealth generation in the Roaring 2020s is uniquely yours, and it begins with these steps. Remember that progress may not always be linear, and setbacks are part of the process. Stay committed to your financial goals, adapt to change, and continue learning. As you implement these strategies and principles, you'll be well on your way to achieving financial success and creating a prosperous future for yourself and your loved ones. The Roaring 2020s are yours to conquer, one step at a time.

Chapter 13: Conclusion - Your Wealth-Building Legacy

As we conclude this journey through the Roaring 2020s and the strategies for wealth generation in this dynamic era, it's essential to reflect on the legacy you're building and the impact your financial success can have on your life and the lives of those around you.

The Power of Wealth Beyond Numbers

While wealth often involves numbers and financial achievements, it also extends beyond monetary measures. Consider the broader impact of your wealth:

Lifestyle Freedom: Wealth can provide the freedom to pursue your passions, spend more time with loved ones, and enjoy life to the fullest.

Philanthropy: As your wealth grows, you have the capacity to make a positive impact on causes and organizations you care about, contributing to meaningful change in your community or the world.

Legacy: Think about the legacy you want to leave behind. How do you want to be remembered? Your wealth-building journey can be a source of inspiration and guidance for future generations.

Balancing Wealth and Well-Being

Wealth generation is not solely about accumulating money; it's also about achieving a sense of well-being and fulfillment. Keep these principles in mind:

Balance: Strive for a balance between financial success and overall well-being. Prioritize physical and mental health, relationships, and personal growth.

Mindfulness: Practice gratitude and mindfulness to appreciate your current financial situation and stay focused on your goals.

Community: Engage with your community and contribute to its growth and welfare. Building connections and giving back can enrich your life.

Continuing the Journey

The journey to wealth generation doesn't end with this book; it's an ongoing pursuit. As you continue your journey, remember these key principles:

Adaptability: Embrace change and stay adaptable. The financial landscape will continue to evolve, and your strategies should evolve with it.

Education: Keep learning and expanding your financial knowledge. Education is a powerful tool in your wealth-building arsenal.

Purpose: Reflect on your values and your "why" for pursuing financial success. Let your purpose guide your decisions and actions.

Resilience: Understand that setbacks are part of any journey. Be resilient and use challenges as opportunities to grow and learn.

Legacy Planning: Consider how your wealth will be passed down to future generations. Estate planning ensures that your legacy aligns with your values and goals.

Your wealth-building journey is a personal and meaningful endeavor. It's not just about accumulating riches but also about creating a legacy, contributing to positive change, and leading a life of purpose and fulfillment. The Roaring 2020s are a unique era filled with opportunities, and you have the tools and knowledge to make the most of it. As you continue on this path, remember that your financial success can be a force for good, shaping a brighter future for yourself and those you care about.